A Beginning-to-Read Book

Let's Play Football

by Mary Lindeen

NORWOODHOUSE PRESS

DEAR CAREGIVER, The *Beginning to Read—Read and Discover* books provide emergent readers the opportunity to explore the world through nonfiction while building early reading skills. The text integrates both common sight words and content vocabulary. These key words are featured on lists provided at the back of the book to help your child expand his or her sight word recognition, which helps build reading fluency. The content words expand vocabulary and support comprehension.

Nonfiction text is any text that is factual. The Common Core State Standards call for an increase in the amount of informational text reading among students. The Standards aim to promote college and career readiness among students. Preparation for college and career endeavors requires proficiency in reading complex informational texts in a variety of content areas. You can help your child build a foundation by introducing nonfiction early. To further support the CCSS, you will find Reading Reinforcement activities at the back of the book that are aligned to these Standards.

Above all, the most important part of the reading experience is to have fun and enjoy it!

Sincerely,

Shannon Cannon

Shannon Cannon, Ph.D.
Literacy Consultant

Norwood House Press • P.O. Box 316598 • Chicago, Illinois 60631
For more information about Norwood House Press please visit our website at
www.norwoodhousepress.com or call 866-565-2900.
© 2016 Norwood House Press. Beginning-to-Read™ is a trademark of Norwood House Press.
All rights reserved. No part of this book may be reproduced or utilized in any form or by any
means without written permission from the publisher.

Editor: Judy Kentor Schmauss
Designer: Lindaanne Donohoe

Photo Credits:

Shutterstock, cover, 6-7 (Arina P Habich),13 (Alexey Stiop), 8, 9 (Action Sports Photography), 14 (Aspen Photo), 14 inset (Aspen Photo), 15 (Richard Paul Kane), 16-17 (Alexi Stiop), 18-19 (Aspen Photo), 24-25 (Aspen Photo), 26-27 (Aspen Photo), 28-29 (Raigl); Dreamstime,1, 4-5 (©Guzmer), 10-11 (©Drx), 12-13 (©AmericanSpirit), 20-21 (©Herreid), 22-23 (©Herreid)

Library of Congress Cataloging-in-Publication Data
    Lindeen, Mary.
    Let's play football / by Mary Lindeen.
        pages cm. – (A Beginning to Read Book)
    Summary: "Football is a team sport that is played on a field. Players wear
uniforms, helmets, pads, and cleats. There are different ways to get points,
and the other team will try to stop you! Find out how to win a game. This
title includes reading activities and a word list"– Provided by publisher.
    Audience: K to Grade 3.
    ISBN 978-1-59953-684-2 (Library Edition : alk. paper)
    ISBN 978-1-60357-769-4 (eBook)
    1. Football–Juvenile literature. I. Title.
    GV950.7.L46 2015
    796.332–dc23
                   2014047623

Manufactured in the United States of America in Stevens Point, Wisconsin. 275N–062015

Many people like football.

Some people like to play it.

Some people like to watch it.

Some people like to do both.

Football is a team sport.

Two teams play each other.

Each team has its own uniform.

Each player has a number.

Players have helmets.
They have pads, too.

These help keep the players safe.

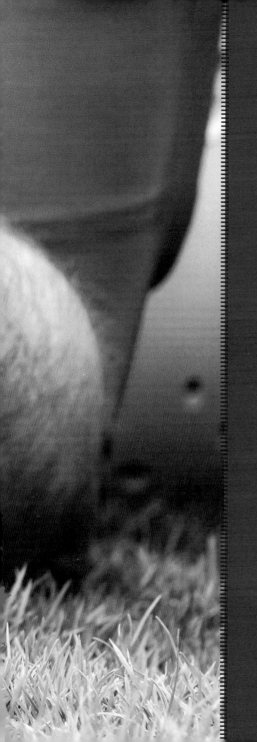

Players also have football cleats.

They help players run better.

The game is played
on a football field.

There is one goalpost
at each end.

13 ...

A football has an odd shape.
You can throw it or kick it.

You can hold it and run with it.

You can get points in different ways.

You can run with the ball to the end of the field.

You can throw the ball to another player at the end of the field.

You can kick the
ball through the
goalposts.

The other team will
try to stop you.

They can even push
you down!

Referees make
sure players
follow the rules.

The game is over.

The team with the
most points wins.

The players did
a good job.

Good game!

·· Reading Reinforcement ··

CRAFT AND STRUCTURE

To check your child's understanding of this book, recreate the following diagram on a sheet of paper. Read the book with your child, then help him or her fill in the diagram using what they learned. Work together to complete the diagram by writing facts and ideas about football in the outer circles:

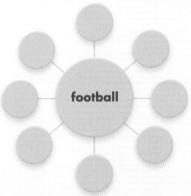

football

VOCABULARY: Learning Content Words

Content words are words that are specific to a particular topic. All of the content words for this book can be found on page 32. Use some or all of these content words to complete one or more of the following activities:

- Have your child think of synonyms (words with similar meanings) or antonyms (words with opposite meanings) for as many content words as possible.

- Create an idea web for the content words. Write a content word in the middle of the diagram. Help your child write related words and ideas in the outer circles.

- Ask your child to use his or her own words to define each of the content words. Have your child use each content word in a sentence.

- Provide clues about the meaning of a content word, and have your child guess the word.

- Help your child make word cards: On each card, have him or her write a content word, draw a picture to illustrate the word, and write a sentence using the word.

FOUNDATIONAL SKILLS: Pronouns

Pronouns are words used in place of nouns (people, places, things, or ideas). Have your child identify which words are pronouns in the list below. Then help your child find pronouns in this book.

some	they	you	help	uniforms
it	football	players	its	team

CLOSE READING OF INFORMATIONAL TEXT

Close reading helps children comprehend text. It includes reading a text, discussing it with others, and answering questions about it. Use these questions to discuss this book with your child:

- What could be a reason for the numbers on uniforms?
- What would happen if players didn't wear helmets or pads?
- What do referees have to do with rules?
- How would you combine football with another sport to create a new game?
- How would you feel if your football team won a game? Lost a game?

FLUENCY

Fluency is the ability to read accurately with speed and expression. Help your child practice fluency by using one or more of the following activities:

- Reread this book to your child at least two times while he or she uses a finger to track each word as you read it.
- Read the first sentence aloud. Then have your child reread the sentence with you. Continue until you have finished this book.
- Ask your child to read aloud the words they know on each page of this book. (Your child will learn additional words with subsequent readings.)
- Have your child practice reading this book several times to improve accuracy, rate, and expression.

··· Word List ···

Let's Play Football uses the 82 words listed below. *High-frequency* words are those words that a[re] used most often in the English language. They are sometimes referred to as sight words becaus[e] children need to learn to recognize them automatically when they read. *Content words* are any word[s] specific to a particular topic. Regular practice reading these words will enhance your child's ability [to] read with greater fluency and comprehension.

High-Frequency Words

a	do	in	on	these
also	down	is	one	they
an	each	it	or	through
and	end	its	other	to
another	even	like	over	too
at	get	make	own	two
both	good	many	people	ways
can	has	most	some	will
did	have	number	the	with
different	help	of	there	you

Content Words

ball	goalpost(s)	pads	safe	try
better	helmets	play(ed, er, ers)	shape	uniform
cleats	hold	points	sport	watch
field	job	push	stop	wins
follow	keep	referees	sure	
football	kick	rules	team(s)	
game	odd	run	throw	

··· About the Author

Mary Lindeen is a writer, editor, parent, and former elementary school teacher. She has written more than 100 books for children and edited many more. She specialize[s] in early literacy instruction and books for young readers, especially nonfiction.

··· About the Advisor

Dr. Shannon Cannon is a teacher educator in the School of Education at UC Davis, where she also earned her Ph.D. in Language, Literacy, and Culture. She serves on the clinical faculty, supervising pre-service teachers and teaching elementary methods courses in reading, effective teaching, and teacher action research.